OPEN DOORS

OPEN DOORS

NEW SELECTED POEMS

Anna Adams

Edited by John Killick

Shoestring Press

All rights reserved. No part of this work covered by the copyright hereon may be reproduced or used in any means – graphic, electronic, or mechanical, including copying, recording, taping, or information storage and retrieval systems – without written permission of the publisher.

Printed by imprintdigital
Upton Pyne, Exeter
www.imprintdigital.net

Typeset by narrator
www.narrator.me.uk
info@narrator.me.uk
033 022 300 39

Published by Shoestring Press
19 Devonshire Avenue, Beeston, Nottingham, NG9 1BS
(0115) 925 1827
www.shoestringpress.co.uk

First published 2014
© Copyright: Anna Adams

The moral right of the author has been asserted.

ISBN 978 1 907356 96 4

CONTENTS

Introduction

Places	**1**
Near Mas De La Dames	3
A River	5
At Douk Ghyll Cave	6
Hebridean Sabbath	7
Scarp Song	8
A Map of the Outer Hebrides 5	9
The Consecration of the House	10
Spring Tide 2	12
Creatures	**15**
Brother Fox	17
The Carpet-Slippered Hare	18
Magpies	20
Otter Letter	21
Cormorants Diving	23
Jizz 1	24
Tortoiseshells Overwintering	25
Worm	26
Wasps' Nest	28
Butterfly Worksong	30
Common Starlings	31
A Sun King with Earth Queens	33
Plants and Trees	**35**
The Sunflowers	37
September, with Grass-of-Parnassus Flowers	39
Flowering Berberis and Bees	41
Rearing Trees in Sheep Country	42
Old Earth Repudiates New Spring	44
The Hospitality of Rowan Trees	46
Flowering Cherry-Orchards	47

People	**49**
Her Dancing Days	51
Mister Jarman's Ghosts	53
Monologue of the Retired Fishing Bailiff	55
Miss Jones	57
Personal	**59**
from A Reply to Intercepted Mail (A Verse-Letter to WH Auden)	61
A Meditation on Some Drawings of Dandelion Seed-Heads	63
The Self Portrait	65
Credentials	67
Dead Letter	69
Grief,	71
Everlasting Expanding Rings 1	72
The Forgetting School 2: School Song	73
Memorials 2: Sailing By	74
The Angel	76
Knocking On	77
Encore	**79**
Mooncycle	81

Poems taken from:

A Reply to Intercepted Mail (Peterloo Poets 1979)
Brother Fox (MIDNAG 1983)
Dear Vincent (Littlewood 1986)
Trees in Sheep Country (Peterloo Poets 1986)
Nobodies (Peterloo Poets 1990)
Island Chapters (Littlewood/Arc 1991)
Life on Limestone (Smith Settle 1994)
Green Resistance: New and Selected Poems (Enitharmon 1996)
A Paper Ark (Peterloo Poets 1996)
Flying Underwater (Peterloo Poets 2004)
Time-Pockets (Fisherrow 2011)

INTRODUCTION

Anna Adams was born in 1926, and died in late 2011. She, and her better-known painter husband Norman, were Londoners, but adopted the North, and spent part of most years over more than five decades at their house Butts at Horton-in-Ribblesdale in North Yorkshire. They also spent substantial periods of time in London, Newcastle-upon-Tyne, the South of France, and on the island of Scarp in the Outer Hebrides. Anna was a good artist but an outstanding poet.

She was a woman of decided opinions, and her essays and articles and voluminous correspondence attest to her ability to give eloquent voice to them. Her poems are decisive and memorable. She didn't like the 'confessional' school, despite writing two long autobiographical poems which teeter on the edge of that category. She distrusted free verse, and described herself as a 'formalist'. She was proficient in the use of rhyme and metre.

Anna wrote with incomparable panache on many subjects, but especially creatures and landscapes. She was a master of descriptive detail, but never let this gift obscure the overall message of a poem. She was also increasingly interested in relationships and wrote many pen-portraits of her relations and the people she came across. So half of this Selected is nature and the other half human nature. She was well-published (five collections with Peterloo, two with Littlewood, a Selected and two edited anthologies with Enitharmon) but never broke through to the national reputation her talent and professionalism deserved. I am confident that she will be valued by future generations.

– John Killick

Places

NEAR MAS DE LA DAMES

Between the green and drunken vines
and silver-grey leaved olive groves,
I walked uphill along a sunbaked track,
looking for a remembered place:
a sunken lane that seemed, last time I came,
to be a bit of England in Provence.
As I approached the corner of that lane
I touched the shallows of a pool of shadow
spread by a forking cypress tree
that grew set back a little from the road.
It wasn't a dark pillar, like the others,
but slant and branchy, making a great roof,
and in its shelter, at a weathered table,
a woman sat and wrote.

    I said 'Bonjour Madame' as she looked up,
and she returned my greeting. I walked by
and found the hidden lane where noonday sun –
glaring through foliage – lit swallowtails
and yellow thistles while the loud cicadas
filed at high cypress bars. It was not England.
It wasn't even cooler than elsewhere.
As I returned, the lady still sat writing
at her ramshackle table in the shade,
like a recording angel, but no spirit;
not allegorical but personal.

    She wore real clothes, not robes: a cotton dress
and, covering grey hair, a light brown scarf
was knotted at her nape. Her bare brown arms
were strong as mine. Her sandals were like mine.
She kept her papers in old cardboard files:
she had no scrolls of parchment, no quill pen,
and, as I passed, her eyes met mine and smiled.
I would have liked to speak, but dared not do so.

What language to begin in? She looked English.
Was she writing a novel? Children's stories?
A treatise on cicadas? Marking devoirs
or working out her income-tax return?
Was she a poet who would keep the world
by power of praise from those who play with fire?
'See this,' she writes, 'and this. Such things are sacred.'
    I would have liked to ask, but dared not speak.
I didn't want to stop her flow of thought,
if she was thinking, or, if she was dreaming,
I didn't wish to wake her, or myself
if I was dreaming a projected self
who sits and writes under a fragrant cypress,
whatever else I may appear to do.
I didn't wish to learn she was a stranger
writing her private letters, not my wise
and ancient muse whose smiling silence blessed me.

A RIVER

Mere water, muttering over inanimate stones,
hemmed between hills and slowly eroded banks
bound by the cordon of trees it undermines,

is nothing a man cannot dam or divert, so he thinks.
Mere water, muttering meaningless syllables,
taking the line of least resistance, slinks

passively downstream, making its road of pebbles
as men made roads by following ambling cattle
between the readymade mountain's limestone tables.

But shallow and muttering water glitters like metal,
knowing itself the cutting-edge of a vast
landscape-carving machine whose work proves fatal

to mountain and valley alike. Millenia past,
its glacier grandfather gouged wide Ribblesdale out
from an exalted plateau of plankton-dust.

These drumlins are glacier-droppings. When thawed out
the ice left a cobbled valley of leaking lakes
that dwindled down to this river that mutters about

the Master of the Cloud-and-Ocean Works
who writes his name in water, so the river
bears the imprimatur that mankind lacks
and prints his changing signature forever.

AT DOUK GHYLL CAVE

I have returned and shall return again,
Summoned by whispering waters to the door
In Penyghent side whence Douk Ghyll is born.

Hundreds of million years 'peine forte et dure'
Have pressed to crush the life from solid seas –
Still living water flows out, cold and clear.

It trickles from the limestone layers that squeeze
Out of their own dead hearts the elixir
That smears them green. The muttering water flows

Under and over stones, through grassy hair,
Stitching together our green world, its thread
Appears and vanishes to reappear,

Shuttling in this secret weaving shed
Where life is spun from stone, and waterfalls
Unravel pools, and comb and card the flood.

This is the source, enfolded by rock walls,
Where trees gather like old wives at a birth,
Of consciousness itself, the voice that calls –

'Though made of stone and rain I'm more than earth'.

HEBRIDEAN SABBATH

Painted with rust, or grey as sea,
one storey, corrugated-tin shacks stay
quiet as limpets at low tide, all day.

The Sabbath closes doors and hushes speech,
manacles hands, gyves feet, suppresses each
workaday wish for play, deserts the beach,

while people from the seashore houses wear
their Sundaybest expressions, oil their hair,
and walk in polished boots to meet their prayer.

Morning till evening, in swept living rooms
of every silent house, they welcome home
the One who made the world, and honour Him.

So, through the week, He, with them in the boats,
pulls in the fish, and grows green crests of oats
in hillside lazybeds. Where far bright floats

mark lobster creels, He lures the prizes in;
always aware of Him, He cares for them,
even in cockleshells tossed by the storm.

And, from steep islands, women frequently
see God out walking on the wrinkled sea,
or, on high ledges where they scythe the hay

He runs in eddies, like a child at play,
on flower-carpets where the hailstones lay.

SCARP SONG

My two strong sons skate out in one small shoe
    treading the polished water
across inverted hills that hang stone heads
among the white clouds in its green glass mirror.

The wind sleeps, and a blanket mist may thicken,
    hiding the polished water,
and no one knows which breathing wind may cloud
the glass, and frost or shiver the green mirror.

All my love's work sits in that far white boat,
    trusting the smiling traitor,
diminishes beyond duststorms of birds.
I see long threads of white hair in the mirror.

My sons ride fearlessly, far out to sea;
    I would not have them other:
they cheat the traitor of his mackerel shoal
and teach the lobster to repent his error.

Northeaster, chase them home; bring rainbow weather
    across the ruffled water.
Confine, Southwest, remorseless water-walls
that travel blind. I dare not name my terror.

A MAP OF THE OUTER HEBRIDES 5

An overall printed with tiny flowers
covers the island woman's turf-brown dress;
the island wears an apron sprigged with stars.

The island woman wears a flowered blouse;
the island uplands wear a heather shawl
dotted with devilsbit and tormentil.

The island woman following her cow
dabbles her hem in raindrenched clover heads;
the island dips its seapink hem in tides.

The island man is carrying a sheep
about his shoulders like a mountain cloud;
the island lads run all about the steep,
gathering their flocks into a crowd.

The sheep flow downhill in a tumbling stream –
men clip them and they fleece the hills for hay,
for Winter comes to shear the flowers away.

The island woman carries memories
of Summer in her apron. When the gale
keens over the dark island, flinging hail,
she answers it with love and lullabies.

THE CONSECRATION OF THE HOUSE

Light, clockwise, at the speed of time,
pans round and makes a time machine
of the synthetic cave dead hands
stacked up to shelter fodder, beast and hind.

Spearshafts of sunlight pierce our rooms;
midwinter noons project bright screens
on whitewashed walls, and bloodshot eyes
of sunsets stare us blind.

Iceblocks of bluish moonlight, stained
by violet snow beyond the sphere
of firelight, tell us, blizzard-bound,
the time when starved hare-shadows gnaw the ground.

This hollow sundial's second hand
wavers, but its inconstancy
has method in it. Sun and moonlight hands
lever this heavyweight, this rooted mound

of stones and all its freight through time:
creating days and months and years
that bear it through the centuries.
Our home's forgotten builders planned

its piercings well. Midwinter sun
shines clear through low-silled windows, but in June
the shadow-mottled light is almost drowned
by layered foliage and frond

and falls in watery patterns where –
some afternoon – the sun's flat footprints hint
that Someone called while passing, found
us out, but left the greeting of a friend.

Light consecrates the house, like love
and time. Here my grown children learned
to walk, and went away. Like sand
dust trickles through this year-glass. Suns wheel round

and pour their photons through my eyes.
Through twenty years of days and nights I've scanned
time's heliographs. Now I respond in kind
with happiness, brief radiance of mind.

SPRING TIDE 2

If England were Japan, the BBC
    would tell us that the foaming tide of May,
       now north of Watford, crossed the Trent today,
and sea-bent hawthorn blooms in Enderby.

The Spring tsunami, thoroughly benign,
    progresses by unbroken waves of hedges
       and tows green seas, all frothy at the edges,
then climbs the Pennines to their plimsoll line.

The blossom reaches Tyneside, creamy white;
    it flowers on Newcastle's wide town moor
       and clings to cliffs on England's north-east shore
whiter than swirling kittiwakes in flight.

It's overtaken Alston, Allendale
    and Blanchland; it wept petals at Tow Law
       (what is that stark abandoned village for?)
It's flooded Otterburn and Holy Isle.

On Lindisfarne there is an avenue
    of Hawthorn trees that lean towards the land
       at forty-five degrees, yet they still stand:
a parallelogram of cows browse through.

In Paradise I hope to sit again
    to finish off the drawing I began
       within those trees before I upped and ran
away to London to oblige my man.

Now jackdaws on the Roman wall declare
    high tide has breached old Hadrian's defences
    and flows through Scotland! I come to my senses
and stop; I am too old to chase it there.

Creatures

BROTHER FOX

Men net the seeming-docile hills
    in mesh of walls, but fail
to kill the fox of the high fells
    who lives beyond the pale.

I trickle under drystone walls
    while staid law-keepers dream,
and creep, when mooncast shadow falls,
    towards the valley farm.

The serpent writhes in my backbone,
    the snake dances in yours,
and treacherously lets me in
    to snap my wanton jaws.

Men load the valley fields with walls
    but still cannot subdue
the bandit of the stony fells
    who lives, deep-earthed in you.

I trot, blood-dark, close by the wall
    under snow-smothered moon,
printing bad news with each footfall
    towards the winking town.

The serpent writhes in my backbone,
    the snake dances in yours,
and hypnotises gentlemen
    into bloodlust and wars.

THE CARPET-SLIPPERED HARE

Dotted and dashed, the indiscreet
    snow broadsheet tells the news
in morse tapped out by long back feet
    and ladylike front paws;
"The carpet-slippered hare grows desperate
    for straws."

Gnawing our cabbage to its root,
    (dropped pellets pay the bill),
he hobbles off, no longer fleet,
    finds nothing left to fill
his belly, levers himself – hunger-light –
    uphill.

While proley rabbits crowd in holes,
    aloof but down-and-out,
Hare sits on fitted carpet-soles
    for comfort. Delicate
front paws scratch snow for grass, but blizzard seals
    his fate.

Hissing and whispering, the sleet –
    past flattened ears, dim eyes –
flies horizontal, cakes his coat,
    but ice lacks calories;
so Hare falls off his ill-assorted feet
    and dies.

Laughing, the undertaker crows
    dismember him, and eat;
but on the piebald hill grass grows
    more green as snows retreat.
There, cantering on well-heeled slipper-toes
    Hares meet.

MAGPIES

One's for sorrow; two appear for joy
to glitter along the edge of a threadbare wood
and overlook the scavenging, riffraff rooks
and sober, industrious jackdaws that walk the field
prodding the mud for food.

More like enormous tropical butterflies
than British birds, they are crows that have won the pools
and wear evening dress all day, so, with springy strut,
they show off satin shirts, white epaulettes,
and iridescent, green and blue silk tails.

With flashy wings they flutter, freewheel, flap,
seem casual, but loiter with intent;
through spyholes in black hoods they case the joint –
this green upholstered landscape – preen and scratch
and wait for singing chickens' eggs to hatch.

Fine feathers make fine crows – mere liar birds –
both lucky and unlucky, like the rest.
Perhaps some gamekeeper could not resist
the target of those guiltless villains' vests;
or have they flown to roost in taller trees

with better views, and built a bonfire nest
such as success deserves? For I have missed
my first and second murderers for days:
now hear them shake their bones, deep in the woods,
haunting, immortal in their shot-silk shrouds.

OTTER LETTER

I knew you at first glance, though far offshore,
disporting in the satin-surfaced sea.
You were no seal – too small and too alert –
you hadn't that forsaken-merman stare
with which seals look at land, as though a man
were bedded in that seamless blubber coat.
You hadn't their blunt, slablike look, but peered
inquisitively, with your pointed head
craning from feline shoulders, at the brash
and shouting perpendiculars that walked.
You looked amazed – amused –
at our impedimenta – rubber boats,
our oars and engines – where, just in your skin,
you're fearlessly, amphibiously at home
and, I suspect, glad not to be a man.
You own the title deeds to rocks and caves:
you've signed the parchment beach. Your tracks confirm
possession. Here you landed, shook yourself
and scratched up sand, and rolled, then wrote along
the lines between obliterating waves
and last saliva splash of lapping tide.
This is an otter beach. Your kind belongs
to seas where we are poor forked aliens –
helpless without those cities at our backs
that make our adaptations to your world.
Insouciant as a cormorant, you dived –
I glimpsed your flank, which curved like a small wave –
and disappeared into your element.
Since then your streamlined joy possesses me,
and leads me on to write.

For all our lacks –
our insulating boots and plastic macs,
sea crutches, sea-bathchairs, and our false limbs –
we humans have some assets. Empathy.
We dive into mind's all-reflecting sea
for images, and words that leave live tracks.

CORMORANTS DIVING

Twin cormorants at swim, which means 'at dive',
    meet only intermittently above
the roof of their cool pantry where, alive,
    they store bright shoals of minnows in the grove
of river-weeds that wave upstream or down
    according to the ebbing/flowing tide.
They take no interest in land-bound man;
    their world is river-shaped, more long than wide,
and only river-deep. They use the sky
    for ritual mating-flights, and are well-schooled
in bird-deportment, tilting small chins high,
    and grooming, keeping plumage preened and oiled.

But their true beings' bliss, their bodies' thought,
is flying underwater, out of sight.

JIZZ 1

Bird-watchers have a necessary word
for distant silhouettes, the shape and stance
of grounded lapwings, or that war-lord bird
the kestrel, and the dipper's curtsey dance
on mossy midstream stones; or – over wide
and tidal Thames – the motionless, erect
grey cipher that means heron at his trade.
For, at a glance, bird-watchers can detect
a species, and their secret is the "jizz",
which word is neither Norse nor Latinate,
and has no truck with Greek and all that jazz.
It was forged out of need to indicate
the jizz, explained above, which all things have:
birds, foxes, hares, and trees; and men I love.

TORTOISESHELLS OVERWINTERING

In my bedroom ceiling's shadiest corner
    a dark encampment of inverted tents
is sitting out the tyranny of Winter.

Like Israelites that keep God's covenants
    in sober arks, or nomad Bedouins
who hide rich mats in fustian tenements,

they fold the magic carpets of their wings,
    concealing hieroglyphics of the meadow
clapped between tatter-bordered coverings.

As dingy as the withered nettlebed,
    as drab as marbled bibles, charred by fire,
or chips of bark or stone, they could be dead

but hang by wiry legs, as fine as hair,
    close-clustered near the plaster desert's edge
like a proscribed religious sect at prayer.

This bivouac preserves the Summer's page
    during eclipse of dandelions and daisies;
it bears pressed sparks of sun through this dark age:

one night between oasis and oasis.

WORM

This drizzle rots white tapes
of wallside snow, thaws out
the earth so that a worm escapes

to probe, with tapered snout,
hard tarmac where it cannot find –
although it gropes about –

the way back underground.
It stretches out its span
of pearl-complexioned, blind

and naked gut, grows thin
and long, and then contracts
its length again.

It seems the fool elects
to cross the rain-wet road
while ignorant of facts

such as: it is thrush-food,
and there are tractor-wheels.
Misguided annelid,

you seem to have two tails
but one's your brainless head.
Unminded grit-canals

should hide beneath the mud:
why not move in reverse
and thus go back to bed

before your plight grows worse?
Its boneless finger points
across a universe

of road, so, all at once,
I seize the creature's saddle.
Convulsed, and lacking joints,

it knots into a muddle
which I set down on grass.
Released from its tight huddle

it burrows. Soon its arse
waves me goodbye, withdraws
to worms' nutritious house:

the home of both of us.

WASPS' NEST

Beneath our lintel hung a papery breast
nippled with penetrating dark that pierced
the layered curtain of the queen wasp's nest.

Out of this Summer palace, princelings flew;
some hunted, some had building work to do;
the population and the palace grew.

They fetched new woodpulp, added paper ridges
and, working backwards along selvages,
turbanned the nest in mummy bandages.

A cabbage with grey leaves, drilled by a worm:
a pendent dome: a tumour on the beam:
a paper brain that hummed with thoughts of home:

the prison chapel of a pregnant nun
who crouched in prayer, walled up from the sun,
to bear her thousand children, one by one.

Her nursery, inverted tree of pods,
has hatched its hundreds, but the queen still adds
more eggs, possessed by summer's dying gods.

The princes' number dwindles. Still tight-laced
and elegant as ever – isthmus waist
links tiger bustle to her pigeon chest –

the venerable queen within the walls
sits brooding over trays of cradle cells
where perfect wasps lie dead beneath their seals.

A secret monument to Summer past,
she dessicates in darkness, grey with dust,
killed by the silent treachery of frost.

BUTTERFLY WORKSONG

To be a butterfly is no light matter;

> with glittering rapidity we flutter
> huge sails like airborne windmills, stop the motor

and drill for nectar wells, then, like blown litter,
we putter off again. We are the porters

> in wild art galleries, and shift exhibits
> from dandelions, or thistle-topmost summits,

to gardens in the humans' walled-in quarters.
Each diptych lifts its labouring transporter

> which, inadvertently in course of duty,
> must pollinate the flowers where, blind to beauty,

we top up fuel tanks of honey-water.
Much put-upon, we batter wings to tatters,

> and if we take time off to understand
> our purposes, the shadow of a hand

destroys our quivering rest. Don't think us flighty;
we dance like sparks to rearrange the weighty

> midsummer exhibition: bear the garden
> on shoulders bowed beneath their gaudy burden

of abstract canvases by the Almighty.

COMMON STARLINGS

About the layered air,
    like locusts, starling-kind
wheel in great flocks above the city square:
    quite leaderless, and yet so disciplined
    they seem to share one mind.

Even the dreaming seer
    remembered starling-kind
as numerous and nameless, in his Hell;
    he saw their dustclouds whirling in the wind
    of lust, borne round and round.

My earth-besotted eyes
    and Dante's are combined
in wonderment at many forming one
    when, instant as the louvres of a blind,
    the birds, to no command,

turn, flashing in the sun.
    Sound instinct is the wind
their undiminished numbers ride through time;
    lust orders doubtful reason jettisoned;
    impulse and action are joined.

Angelic privates drill
    for bloodless wars, descend
by corporate and democratic will,
    fill leaftiled sycamores with squealing sound,
    survey their feeding ground,

then raid our rowantree
> whose burdened boughs extend
bloodscarlet berry clusters, offered free
> to chatterers and flutterers who lend
> excited twigs, at Summer's end,

brief foliage of wings.

A SUN KING WITH EARTH QUEENS

The metallic cough of the coppery King-in-exile
heralds the pheasants' arrival, requests our attention
although he has nothing to say but 'Look at me, look
at the burnished scales of my soft, ceremonial armour,
the springy plumes of my cantilevered tail
and gold-buttoned armistice poppies on either cheek; observe
my priestly collar and sea-green cowl
but do not notice my modestly camouflaged Queens.'

During our absence, one morning, he dropped us a feather;
its chestnut filaments had been dipped in sunlight
though, near its root, it was grey with thermal down.
This gold-tipped message informed us that he had called.
Twice daily he ushers his shy harem through our reeds;
his seven furtive princesses in brown-speckled tweeds
consider that ours is a safe house. Increasingly silent,
we bang few doors and fail to mow our lawns.

Perched on the topmost rail of our shaky fence,
the resplendent King proclaims a palace-garden
of coltsfoot beds, and hedges spread into thickets;
his dowdy Queens nod automatic approval,
pecking at mosses between wild raspberry canes.
If I go out with the washing, I beg their pardon,
conceding squatters' rights to the Wilderness,
and title deeds to the Royal Concubines.

Dappled with sunspots, deep in the undergrowth,
they crouch, disguised as shadows or drifts of leaves,
and brood over crucibles full of the Royal Genes.
The gilded King steps out and coughs, midfield,
to draw the fire of our attention: 'Look
at my Eldorado armour, my glaring eyes
buttoning blood-petalled poppies for brothers you killed;
my Queens are restoring the dead in their time-machines.'

Plants and Trees

THE SUNFLOWERS

With laiking southerners' extravagance
    I sowed this northern hill with sunflowerseed
though sighing ash and thorn might scorn the dance
    of heliotropic-tilting leaf and head.

I shivered in my exile, (Spring delayed),
    and longed to grow tall vegetable suns,
an infant god's flame bonnet, self-portrayed:
    a troupe of haloed clowns.

Devotedly I watered, through May's drought,
    twin cotyledons, cunningly tugged out
of splitting husks, to balance on one foot
    and juggle with the light.

They drank, through June, the grey incessant rain
    and fed their cordate rags on cold and wet;
by twos and threes, leaves clambered toward noon
    long after noon, and no bloom budded yet.

None flowered when September gales laid waste;
    reclined, oblique, my solar totems lay:
but each raised a defiant, green-clawed fist,
    and each fist held an eye.

These spiky hands were heads, and all their minds
    were compound lenses, wrapped in eye-lash fringe,
till straight through Winter's ruined borderlands
    a south wind breathed on each stiff petal-hinge.

> Slowly they splash the dusk with wheels of flame
> > to bear me through the dark; grave offerings:
> coronas of eclipse, at curfew time:
> > the tattered paper crowns of beggar kings.

SEPTEMBER, WITH GRASS-OF-PARNASSUS FLOWERS

Raddled and blowsy, fruitladen hat askew,
Ceres no longer cares for appearances;
her gait is a little unsteady but she has come through

Summer's enormous task. Her abundances –
crocheted cell by cell from the mineral earth
and sunlight – are all but completed, so Ceres dances

homeward to sleep it off. Since Spring's first milktooth
snowdrop, she's been on call for unfolding, in situ,
buds within buds, birds, bugs; as ubiquitous midwife

delivering Summer's goods. Now, solid as statues,
masses of leathery leaves model trees into weighty
monuments to inventive and fecund virtue.

The windless air is an overpopulous city,
dusty with hoverers, hoovered forever by swallows.
Surplus lapwings and jackdaws eddy like litter.

Ceres can't go a step further; complacent and mellow,
she sits in a hedge, overdressed in scarlet beads,
smiling at gypsy ragwort's tarnishing yellow,

laughing at disarray of her carnival weeds.
Rosebay willowherb's last pink steeplejack petals
wave from their leaning spires in a blizzard of seeds.

Emptied, and thereby fulfilled, the goddess settles
down for a doze, drops off and begins to snore,
happy to die in this ditch among knapweed and nettles,

renouncing Olympus and the repeated chore
of turning stones into bread. She just can't face
decking old Earth in eternal youth once more.

Spiders veil the sleeping old woman in lace;
mists creep down from the mountains and spirit her bones
away, beyond vanished horizons, and leave in her place

sacred albino buttercups, signed with green veins.

FLOWERING BERBERIS AND BEES

I am a world, the only world I know,
though humming outer-space ships visit me
with cryptic messages. They come and go

tickling suggestively. Like yellow snow
my loosened garments fall continuously
from canopy to earth. From space I know

I grope towards blue summer air; I grow
while tenor angels sing of mystery
and probe my roses as they come and go.

If there are other trees that blossom so,
whose sulphur buds unfold successively,
then others know the ecstasy I know.

The spineless goosegrass clambers from below
where gold confetti-drifts turn brown and dry,
but still the humming space-ships come and go

to milk my last pale virgin's honey-flow
and murmur to each swelling ovary
of other worlds I cannot know
though humming outer-space-ships come and go.

REARING TREES IN SHEEP COUNTRY

Sheep are tree-wolves. Even the hare attacks
    in snow, and gnaws the bark far from the ground,
        recording heights of drifts, but seldom rings trees round
and doesn't hunt the rooted flock in packs.

But in late February, belly's trouble
    drives the sheep wild. Though bulging big with lamb
        they scramble over walls and topple them.
Where one stone falls, soon a wide gate of rubble

welcomes the eager rabble. Our young trees
    are sweet as sugar-sticks with rising sap,
        and tempt the sheep as a self-service shop
tempts children. Rubber lips stretch up and seize

horse-chestnut toffees, tear smooth twigs of beech
    whose curving fingers beckon towards Spring;
        grey mouths emulsify mute promising
of intricately folded summer speech.

Down from cropped hills – short backs and sides and tops
    trimmed by the nibbling jaws of ruminants
        maintaining level status for all plants –
the wandering columns of stiff-legged mops

leak like spilt suds through gaps and over stiles,
    by mazy ways towards out tufted croft.
        Now there is scarcely one unscarred tree left;
tooth-chiselled wood shines out as white as skulls

from rowan bark, from sturdy apple boles;
    even the thorn has lost some finial buds.
    Trees grow so slowly, unlike visioned woods
that spring from magic beans. Two chestnuts are flayed poles.

And in the pearly evening light, like bosses
    studding the dewy field, the sheep lie, mild
    as though the wolf and lamb were reconciled,
but we lament fresh wounds and total losses.

While grass renews its inch, we come to terms
    with less than leafy symmetry, now clipped,
    imperfect, vulnerable, and accept
long guardianship begun in carefree games.

OLD EARTH REPUDIATES NEW SPRING

Flowers are not budding under my skin.
I wrap old Autumns about me – torn raincoats of leaves –
to hide this absurd petal-plumage. It's none of mine.
Above me the rocks draw level and regular graphs
across grey sky, thus proving all normal for March.
Perhaps the spinney's topmost boughs need oil;
small squeaky birds, migrating in restless flocks,
cling, high up, with feet like prehensile twigs.
The treecreeper's steep, erratic chart of his climb
up spindly trunks, and swift, oblique flight down,
records no abnormal fever. Unheard tree-hearts
pump sapwood green with health. The pulse of the beck
where, passively, water ticks steadily out of the moss,
is calm. No white spate thunders.
Those twisted thorns are anemographs of spent gales;
their dryads are bent old women
and no god moans with desire in their arms any more.
And yet I cannot pretend these petals are snow,
though fieldfare flocks still feed on muckspread fields.
A clockwork wagtail moves among dung-caked cows,
newly evicted from shippons, with staggering calves
that must have tasted the Spring's illicit still,
like the drunk and disorderly lapwings. But I have not.
Clear cold water seeps through my mossy veins.
I have seen too many winters to be deceived.
The sycamore carries too many green birthday flames,
but the black-tipped ash betrays no joy. Nor I –
though codpiece buds may burst on red stemmed sallows.
At each twig-end green mercury breaks the glass.
I am nurse to a lovesick nature, untouched myself,
all antibody, immunised time after time;
my response to lovesongs is rook-raucous scorn.
(These petals are coincidental.) Hardbitten, twice shy

to expose any impulse again to the merciless sky,
snatch my dun overall closer, to hide
sap-veined and bride-white flowers, but it has frayed
to silky fringes of luminous green
as vivid as I would be drab. How could I know –
when the south wind blew and the sun shone out of the cloud –
that so little kindness could warm and transform me, persuade
my case-hardened crust so often and reveal
these sun-reflecting eyes, these trembling tongues,
this shameless calyx of scarlet and gold. I bloom
from frosted lips, and love in my own name.

THE HOSPITALITY OF ROWAN TREES

That summer-long slow burn of mountain ashes
prepares a feast. Light blossom-froth was starters
but the main course, dragging the pliant twigs
earthward with heaviness, is berry-clusters
cooked to come-hither scarlet. Guests arrive.
Pot-shaped wood pigeons agitate the leaves
with flutterings and gluttony, and blackbirds
tabletalk and food-call, sotto voce,
while balancing on lithe unstable perches
and picking fruit precisely, with neat beaks.
They eat for weeks but do not strip the tree.
The starling squadrons do that in one day.
Gatecrashers spread the word, and avid flocks
pour out of nowhere, fill the tree with wings
and put an end to hospitality.

The festive baubles, painted by the sunlight
with many coats of colour as they grew:
green, brown, tan, orange, deeper orange, scarlet;
all luminous with warm ingested rays,
are lost, the feast for human eyes reduced
to tired and dowdy salad of green leaves.
This was not rape or theft but deed of gift;
not altruism either; but exchange.
The Rowan casts its bread upon the air –
red pellets gulped by gullets, crushed in crops –
in reciprocity. The tree provides
wages for seed-dispersing foresters
who feed, and scatter future Rowan trees.
Losing its life to save it, nature gives;
the principle is generosity.

FLOWERING CHERRY-ORCHARDS

Quickly, paint the cherry-blossom snow
    before it melts, before the shining masses
that cling to cherry branches all let go
    and fling confetti drifts among the grasses.

Quickly, however clumsy, say some word
    before the blossom scatters make some mark
with brush or chalk on paper, to record
    the transitory light from sooty bark.

Listen, the humming bee-swarms undermine
    unpollenated, wind-resistant power,
and budding leaves contaminate with green
    the silver-whiteness of the virgin flower.

Too late: the vandal wind already blows
    out all the flames of twice-ten-million tapers;
prosaic leaves usurp the orchard boughs
    and we are left with scarred and blotted papers.

People

HER DANCING DAYS
or 'The Death of Mantovani Set Her Off'

(from 'The Spoken Poems of Elizabeth Winifred Rose')

Those old tunes take me back. I used to go
to dances every Saturday. Of course
I wasn't never going to give it up,
and nor was Lily Cannon, but we did.
We wasn't taught, we just picked up the steps.
In summer there was dances in Brent Park;
they called them 'flannel dances': out of doors.
The men could wear grey flannels, not the girls.
I used to make my dresses, buy the stuff
up Cricklewood, and sew them in a day.
I liked the winter evening dances best,
and used to dance with Horace – he was tall,
and we danced well together – Percival –
he was a butler, rather serious –
Jack Roach, Jack Young, and I forget who else:
but there was one I used to like, and then
one Saturday he wasn't there, and I
was heartbroke. Then he wrote.
I was to meet him at the Bald Faced Stag
one Sunday afternoon. We'd never met
by day. I didn't like the looks of him.
And Horace was engaged. Then, at a fair
with Lil, she was all out for a good time,
we met these two. One of them wore a cap.
I don't like caps. 'I'll have him then,' said Lil:
all four slid down the helter-skelter, then
the heel come off me shoe; I had to hop;
he fixed it for me. Later, we arranged
to meet again next evening at the Hyde.
 Lily come round, and sat down by the fire
to knit. 'I'm going out,' I said; 'You're not,

it's raining.' But I was. I had to go.
We didn't know each other's names,
or where we worked, or any thing.
And there he waited for me, in the wet,
and fifty years began.
    I said I'd never give up dancing, and
he said the same of football, but we did;
and Lily gave up dancing too, quite soon.
    We was both seventeen.

MISTER JARMAN'S GHOSTS

Don't you find it creepy, Missis Adams?
I feel it on them stairs: a sort of coolness;
and you fly up and down quite quick, I notice.
I used to do the same myself, but now
Old Annie Domino has slowed me down.
    I started here on night security,
and one night, after midnight, on that landing,
I met a lady. She was very small,
not five foot high, dressed in old-fashioned clothes.
She said, 'Who are you? Tell me who you are.'
She had a small, high, strangled sort of voice:
old and far off. I didn't tell her nothing.
Then once, in the front hall, Sir Allan Grant
glided towards me in a haze of smoke.
That's how you tell it's them. They come through smoke,
and it's all dark behind them, spangled like
with Christmas glitter. He was like his bust.
And then, by day, I saw another lady.
I couldn't see her face but saw her dress
had lots of little buttons, glass, or diamonds.
She walked away with quick but tiny steps –
like this. An old chap told me I had seen
the woman who kept house when he was young.
'You got her to a tee,' he said. Quite often
up in the Private Rooms, I seen a shadow.
It moves across the windows, and I've heard –
down by Nun's Walk – a scream like someone murdered.
Then someone set a tape-recorder up
outside the restaurant, and left it running,
recording all the noises of the night:
the pipes and groaning fridges, then this scream.
They got it on the tape: a woman screaming.
    One night, down in the vaults, one tapped my shoulder.

I turned, and there was no one. I'm a psychic.
The lady from the Psychical Research
said I was Extrasensitive. My Mother
would give what she could spare to those in trouble.
She was religious. I'm a seventh child.
That's why I got this gift. I see and hear them.
    Haven't you seen one, Missis Adams?

MONOLOGUE OF THE RETIRED FISHING BAILIFF

(i.m. Mark Thompson)

Don't talk to me of books: I never read one.
I learn things manually, you know,
he said, twisting his fingers. I don't read,
nor watch the television. If I can't
see things wi' my own eyes I do wi'out.
Nay, books has never been much use to me;
nor newspapers, nor holidays. My wife
insisted, once, and she arranged it all:
a holiday at Morecambe for us both.
What's this? I said, when she packed up my clothes.
We tek the train to Morecambe in the morning.
We never do, I said. We do, she said,
and she were right. She'd booked a week in lodgings.
I couldn't tek to it. It weren't for me;
so I went out next morning, after breakfast,
and saw a bus to Hornby, and I took it,
then walked to Kirkby Lonsdale, got a lift
to Ingleton, but missed the evening bus,
so walked home by moonlight. I were tired
but happier' wi' every step I took.
When I got in, Police was at the door:
your wife raised the alarm; thought you was lost.
I was, but I'm not now, I said; not now.
So after that she took the holidays,
and even went abroad, but I stop home.
I know the river, Ribblehead to Settle;
I know the becks, I know the roads and lanes –
for wasn't I the roadman once? – I know
the Tarn, and all the folk about the valley,
and many in yon graveyard. I remember

the man who built the walls on yonder fell.
He worked alone, for years, out on the mountain
with sheep and hares and skylarks, and the kestrel.
And he could read the sky, and so can I,
and I can read the ground and learn the news
of mushrooms, mink, and when the osprey comes.
I can read well enough, but not in books.
Don't talk to me of books. Tell me you've seen
the kingfisher, or tell me that the otters
have took up residence wi' us again.

MISS JONES

The lady who cooks in the station carpark corner
is having a difficult morning. I hear from some distance
a screaming as though an overexcited macaw –
trained by more than commonly foulmouthed pirates
during long years at sea with never a sighting
of even as much as a female manatee –
were cursing the wintry skies of rainladen cloud.

Can the tenants of new low-cost redbrick
and minimal housing on the Paradise Project
have moved in already to lower the tone of the district?
I wonder, rounding the corner of Eden Road.
 Would there be blood on the tarmac? But it's only Miss Jones
hurling hailstorms of crusts to her vermin hens,
(for "Somebody has to feed them"), shrieking meanwhile –
"Hideous smelly old woman, filthy old tart…"
and words my pen is far too chaste to report.
Are you alright, Miss Jones? I ask her as I pass her.
"Don't bother me now. Piss off. I have troubles enough,"
she shouts, and continues tirading. I walk to the station,
past her Ford in its shroud of tattered sheeting,
parked in the gutter, immobile outside number nine
where her parents died and deserted their blue-eyed daughter
to manage her life as best she could, and she failed
to pay the rent or the rates or the bills for heating
until she was, under protest, evicted. She swore
never to move away from her childhood's front-door.

So there she stays, tucked up in her tin box motor,
cooking her camp-fire meals in the carpark corner,
hanging her washing to dry on the station gateway,
wearing serendipitous layers of clothing
and bringing down, by some thousands, property prices.

When I return from the station, and re-cross the carpark,
she hails me as she carries her stew-bucket home
and asks if she was rude to me in the morning.
"Sometimes I must give vent to my feelings," she says
in ladylike accents, and I nod in answer.
"People get ill if they don't show their feelings; she smiles
a six-year-old's gaptoothed smile, like a witchy child.
"We are warned against bearing false witness; we shouldn't pretend
so I let it all out," she explains. Yes, I understand.
Once she was somebody's cossetted blue-eyed girl
then she was nobody, out in the cold
and telling her tale to the pigeons and stone-deaf sky;
unloading the hurt she suffered. I can understand –
and most of her old-time neighbours try to be kind.

For she is our lady of less than minimal housing,
she is our lady who bows to a living fire;
she is our lady of crusts for the oil-puddle pigeons
and she is our lady who binds up her swollen red feet
in cardboard, paper and tape; and she is our lady
who, when she can bear it no longer – our scarecrow lady –
flings her defiance and scorn at the swift grey sky
full of applauding wings.

Personal

from A REPLY TO INTERCEPTED MAIL (A VERSE-LETTER TO WH AUDEN)

...I read a lot, I wrote a bit, I thought –
    but disconnectedly – I worked for cash;
I drew, I made small sculptures, and I taught,
    and had acquired two children when the crash
    from happiness, the lash of Nemesis,
dropped me from sunlight – woman's summertime –
to punishment – it seemed – for lack of crime.

I'm trying to be honest and extract
    the essence of what happened from events;
to winnow grains of truth from chaff of fact
    and not pretend to feeling or to sense
    more than is mine – nor claiming innocence.
But back in nineteen-sixty, suddenly
shipwrecked into the Leeds Infirmary –

on the receiving end of pity, ill,
    humiliated, and afraid to die –
I dreamed that on my cottage window-sill
    there crawled a captive Brimstone Butterfly
    that battered at the room's impervious eye
with frantic wings, to reach the sun outside,
while all the time the door stood open wide...

* * *

...this is how last year was spent. I made
    a clay Madonna, some ceramic tiles,
and birds and beasts for which I have been paid.
    I must have cooked at least four hundred meals
    and rolled ten thousand miles on racing wheels

as well as reading Dante. Women's days
are usually splintered twenty ways..

I cannot cast out Martha from my heart.
    My family would starve, and garbage fill
the kitchen. Mary chose the better part;
    and Mary listens, Mary can sit still:
but tides of dirt rise to the window-sill
if Martha does not care for many things.
She also serves who serves; and also sings.

Superiority of Mary's state
    lies in that it is chosen. Slavery
takes virtue out of work, love turns to hate
    under compulsion, and sly thievery
    makes generosity seem miserly.
What Martha does we must do to survive,
so Mary may delight in being alive…

A MEDITATION ON SOME DRAWINGS OF DANDELION SEED-HEADS

Over ten years ago I made these marks –
brain-shadows of recurring shapes
that reappear each year, though light wind strips
scarred bases of the anchored rocket-ships
and carries seed far from the parent stalk
to settle on new sites and germinate.
They should have multiplied to numberless
brassyfaced weeds whose origin was here
in this ancestral spheroid's fluffy hair.
This was the worn-out and abandoned world
ten generations, scattered far afield,
have quite forgotten that they left behind.

I made these marks in Summer, sixty-nine.
My mother stayed with us. Our living-room
contained my sons and the demanding screen
that barters shadows for our time, and her
transfixed by spacemen walking on the moon.
I turned my back, but Granny and the boys
gawped at expensive hardware and stuffed guys
while I made drawings of an earthbound weed
whose aeronauts know annual success
probing the wastes. But did my mother guess
her own, inevitable, commonplace
yet awful journey into space drew near?

The seventies, on which we close the door,
were not for her. My first quite parentless
orphaned decade has whitened my brown hair,
so I resemble, in more ways than one,
those dandelions. Blown about a world
or universe of universities

my two young shock-heads seek a rooting bed
while my head ripens possibilities
of potent, breathborne seed, from inner space
where time stands still, though nearer, by ten years,
are our own journeys to untrodden stars
and the obituaries we may not read.

THE SELF PORTRAIT

I thought to draw my living mask,
    with lines, or light and dark,
so propped a glass up on my desk
    and made a charcoal mark.

But in the ground below my room –
    deep in the shadow-well –
a narrow desert longed to bloom
    and so I left my cell

and softly, down the spiral stair,
    crept to a bolted door
and, stepping out into the air,
    proceeded to explore.

Laurels intensified the shade;
    I pruned and thinned, then found
green ferns, and planted more, I made
    small areas of ground

by prising up the trodden stones
    and digging deep; I fed
manure, dried blood and crumbled bones
    into the barren bed

then sought out flowers to make bright
    the semidarkness; most
were toxic as the aconite
    or pallid as a ghost,

but all took root and grew. Pale fire
    shone in the gloom; bile-green
proliferated; nightshade bore
    black phials of atropine.

The belladonna that arrests
    man's heart, grew tall and thrived,
and henbane, on forbidden lists
    of killers, I reprieved.

When I had climbed the secret stair
    and sat again, and drew,
my smiling likeness hinted where
    the true self-portrait grew.

CREDENTIALS

Through the long telescope of thirty years
I see a stoneware bowl, perched on a table.
I had glanced up from reading, saw this crater
balanced on one foot, a flower of clay
brimful of light.

A few days later my young schoolboy son
swung his batwing raincoat round his shoulders
and swept the bowl from tabletop to floor.
It shattered, but its image stayed intact
in time's vacated room.

My son is now the parent of a child
called Ammar, meaning – He that shall not die.
I see him with clear eye: he is adopted;
his features are not blurred by likenesses
to this or that relation.

He stood between the knees of my grown son
and he appeared to me a shining man,
naked of his body, in his soul;
his constant self, complete from the beginning;
the self he would unfold.

And, one winter evening, my old love –
my dear old love who had begun to die –
was sitting by the fireside, half asleep
or thinking, with his face propped on his hand,
and he was young again.

He looked as he did fifty years ago.
His pouchy face was ironed out, uncrumpled;
his widely spaced, imaginative eyes
were full of thought, or dream. If I was dreaming,
my tenderness was real

as that I felt when we were setting out
with both our lives a mountain road before us.
We drove tall morning shadows on ahead,
trod on dark dwarfs at noon, and trailed behind us
tired shadows stretched by sunset

and then we bivouacked in woods or fields,
and one another's arms. But that was then.
We made such journeys: Cornwall, Wales and Ireland,
the Hebrides, our children, middle age,
till we arrived, white-haired,

at now. But those times live, coiled in the present
or rolled in an embroidered bale called Past:
a tapestry to hang across the sky
one day when all is simultaneous.
I've had mad glimpses of it.

DEAD LETTER

1

I pick no bones with death;
endless supply of breath
would be a worse design.
Death is benign.

I throw no stones at time.
It is the spacious room
roofed by a stormy sky
in which we learn to fly.

I have not shed one tear,
my eyes are desert dry;
nor have I yet, my dear,
quite said Goodbye

because, towards the end,
my dearest lifelong friend,
you could no longer hear;
you were not there.

2

Disease is like a worm
that robs us from within
of what makes up a man:
good humour, kindness, dream;

all notions, words, all skill:
only the will to be
stripped of all courtesy
torments us still

till our last energy
escapes with our last breath.

I pick no bones with death.

GRIEF,

but also relief
at being set free of an Angry Old Man of the Sea
who had at last dismounted, or lurched off
from my shoulders where he had perched
so lightly as a stripling years before.
I am no longer his donkey. I straighten up
and look about me, thinking uncensored thoughts.
I need no longer hide my separate mind,
for I am free of his bridle
and his mistaken conception that I am his mother.
When I had children he wanted to be one too,
so he mutated into the difficult eldest:
the jealous one. And when the children were grown
(but after some carefree years of comradeship)
he grew down backwards, to a mansized infant;
white-haired and angry – and who can blame him for this? –
because of his increasing helplessness.
I should have left him on somebody-else's doorstep
and ridden away on the shoulders of a toy-boy.
But I was restrained by that painful thing called love.

EVERLASTING EXPANDING RINGS 1

I found in August, after he died,
hidden in a snowy-flowered bush
a dunnock's nest. Its open cup,
bound fast to twigs, and neatly made
of roots and moss, was lined with silver hair.
This was so smoothly-laid and silky-soft
it could have been newclipped
and dropped that day onto the sunwarmed flags
outside the kitchen door. He hated barbers;
and so he sat there on a stickbacked chair,
a towel round his shoulders, and I snipped –
inexpertly – the fine thinning hair,
once thick and brown, and dropped it there
in summer after summer. More than comfort,
it gives almost unseemly joy
to see those wisps recycled in a cradle.

THE FORGETTING SCHOOL 2: SCHOOL SONG

We're all enrolled in the forgetting school –
The Wintergarden Adult Kindergarten –
where we unlearn our learning, every skill,
till even alphabets are quite forgotten.
At our first kindergartens we wrote down
our names, surnames and all, and got them right.
Here we are Rose, Elizabeth and John;
addresses disappear in fading light.

We learned with pride, and strove to come out top:
now we forget, with rage, our hard-won knowledge,
although our goal is mind's vacuity.
Old arguments repeat themselves, and stop,
while words escape like cagebirds from this college
or School of Ultimate Equality.

MEMORIALS 2: SAILING BY

Half-past-midnight's music, "Sailing By"
heralds the weather-warnings for trawlermen,
yachtsmen, tankers, lonely ocean-rowers
pondskating over unmapped water-dunes
in areas like Rockall, German Bight.
Then "Coastal waters" traces a top-heavy chart
of squat, square-headed Britain, sitting hard
on Kent and Sussex, hatching the Isle of Wight,
bathing its Cornish feet in Atlantic suds
and hugging Wales to its narrow chest, while Ireland
swims away to the West.

I could chant a limited personal list
of seaside stations: Selsey Bill, Southend,
Felixstowe, Sutton-on-Sea, St Margaret's Bay;
then Leiston, Filey, Swanage, Lulworth Cove –
to map my childhood summers.
War was hiatus. Bardsey, Lindisfarne,
then Inishmore, and Scarp in the Hebrides
where I first heard that music – "Sailing By" –
as I enjoyed my late-night fireside bath
while southwest gales rocked house and boat and bay
and all the rest to sleep.

The Hebrides are twenty years away
but that unchanging half-past-midnight tune
still makes our long-abandoned sheiling rise
around me and enclose me, instantly.
Soft tilley-lamplight shows me wooden walls –
tongued and grooved – the painted vertical grain

rivering upward, swerving round dead-wood eyes.
Our looted, or else beachcombed, bric-a-brac –
flat-irons, gannet-skulls, wild flowers in jars
crowd the shelf above the stove
backed by the pinned-up map of Scotland's rocks.

Juniper Horizontalis's rickety bones –
twisted by wind – sprawl on the dresser-top.
Above, on a shelf, four blue enamel plates
like portholes, and – of utilitarian beauty –
four thick white army-surplus porage bowls.
In a drawer, my inherited tin of needles and thread,
scissors and suchlike, holds my mother's ghost –
imprisoned air of home – and on the walls
paintings of sea, and mountains in the sea,
and one of an ultramarine and scarlet lobster
such as my sons braved drowning for, most mornings.

The sisal matting filters white sea-sand,
not dust, and the dying fire would smell of peat,
not coal, if it hadn't gone out; and the stripe of light
beneath the bedroom door has gone out too
with a sigh from the pressure lamp, as "Sailing By"
sailed by and arrived at silence.
The phantom house collapses along with the island,
sinking fathoms down in the foaming sea,
drowning my mother's old tin with her mending gear
decades deep in the past. Unreachable, now,
is the coffined air that used to transport me home.

THE ANGEL

I stayed in all day for the Angel
    who promised to call. He said – Wait:
so I dressed up demurely and waited
    but no angel perched on my gate.

I left doors and windows wide open
    so, whether on foot or in flight
on Miltonic wings, fanning fragrance,
    or if he was beamed down as light,

he shouldn't be able to miss me;
    his angelic greeting would bless,
his quivering wings would caress me,
    his fingers unbutton my dress.

But no angel came all the morning,
    only some twittering birds,
and no angel came before sundown
    though butterflies scribbled some words

in white and invisible writing,
    across empty air, to decode:
Don't idle there, passively waiting:
    try the live lad down the road.

KNOCKING ON

Past fifty, past that five-barred gate
    I shall not climb again,
my dazzled eyes appreciate
    the beauty of young men.

When I was in my upper teens
    and looked in young men's eyes
I saw, reflected in each lens,
    my beauty, shrunk in size

but full of power. I sensed the awe
    that fed my vanity
but when I too felt their desire
    my power drained from me.

Past seventy, I still revere
    the beauty of the young
but know that it must disappear
    like mine, before too long,

into a crumpled parchment bag
    with hair turned grey, or white;
and sight of pantaloon, or hag,
    kills Eros dead with fright.

So we are left with Agape –
    let all the mirrors shiver –
look outward, active empathy
    translates the sensual fever:

> but sometimes, still, the young men leap
>   across dream's five-barred gate
> and Eros frolics through my sleep –
>   so late in life, so late!

Encore

MOONCYCLE

Albino eyelash, or an incomplete
empty parenthesis, before the night
has come of age you sink down, out of sight,
as foundering sail, then whiskertail of light.

Your shadow acorn in its silver cup
absorbs light from your slender crescent line
that thickens nightly, swells to oval, then
becomes a perfect disc. You have grown up.

From dusk to dawn you soar above the dark
steep shadow-cone of Earth. Though you may race
through clouds that smudge, then polish, your bright face,
it takes twelve hours, and more, to draw your arc.

Each evening later, lesser, you arise
till midnight greets you snapped in half, and day
pursues and overtakes, eats all away;
then evening's eyelash takes us by surprise.